Recipes
Blank Cookbook

Recipes

Fill in and organize your favorite recipes to create your own cookbook. Now you can save all your favorite recipes in one handy book! This blank recipe book allows you to write in and organize your personal recipes.

All your favorite keepsake recipes, clipped recipes from the newspaper or magazines that are stored in a drawer can be written down in your own personal recipe book for easy access. Its simplicity and ease of use makes it useful and fun.

Create your own cookbook! Keep all your favorite recipes in one handy place.

This recipe keeper will be just what you need to create something uniquely your own or give as a gift to your children or grandchildren. Never lose or misplace precious recipes again.

Appetizers

Recipe Name: _____

Oven Temp: _____ Cook Time: _____

Ingredient List:

_____   _____

_____   _____

_____   _____

_____   _____

_____   _____

_____   _____

_____   _____

_____   _____

_____   _____

_____   _____

Recipe Directions:

Recipe Name: _____

Oven Temp: _____ Cook Time: _____

Ingredient List:

_____   _____

_____   _____

_____   _____

_____   _____

_____   _____

_____   _____

_____   _____

_____   _____

_____   _____

_____   _____

Recipe Directions:

Recipe Name: _____

Oven Temp: _____ Cook Time: _____

Ingredient List:

_____   _____

_____   _____

_____   _____

_____   _____

_____   _____

_____   _____

_____   _____

_____   _____

_____   _____

_____   _____

Recipe Directions:

Recipe Name: _____

Oven Temp: _____ Cook Time: _____

Ingredient List:

_____   _____

_____   _____

_____   _____

_____   _____

_____   _____

_____   _____

_____   _____

_____   _____

_____   _____

_____   _____

Recipe Directions:

Recipe Name: _____

Oven Temp: _____ Cook Time: _____

Ingredient List:

_____   _____

_____   _____

_____   _____

_____   _____

_____   _____

_____   _____

_____   _____

_____   _____

_____   _____

_____   _____

Recipe Directions:

Recipe Name: _____

Oven Temp: _____ Cook Time: _____

Ingredient List:

_____   _____

_____   _____

_____   _____

_____   _____

_____   _____

_____   _____

_____   _____

_____   _____

_____   _____

_____   _____

Recipe Directions:

Recipe Name: _____

Oven Temp: _____ Cook Time: _____

Ingredient List:

_____   _____

_____   _____

_____   _____

_____   _____

_____   _____

_____   _____

_____   _____

_____   _____

_____   _____

_____   _____

_____   _____

Recipe Directions: _____

Recipe Name: _____

Oven Temp: _____ Cook Time: _____

Ingredient List:

_____   _____

_____   _____

_____   _____

_____   _____

_____   _____

_____   _____

_____   _____

_____   _____

_____   _____

_____   _____

_____   _____

Recipe Directions:

Cooking Terms

Bake
To cook in the oven. The cooking of food slowly with gentle heat, causing the natural moisture to evaporate slowly and concentrating the flavor.

Basting
To brush or spoon liquid fat or juices over meat during roasting. Adds flavor and will prevent it from drying out.

Batter
A mixture of flour, fat and liquid that is thin enough in consistency to require a pan to encase it. Used in such preparations as cakes and some cakes.

Beat
To smooth a mixture by briskly whipping or stirring it up with a spoon, fork, wire whisk, rotary beater or electric mixer.

Bind
To thicken a sauce or hot liquid by stirring in ingredients such as eggs, flour, butter or cream.

Blackened
A popular Cajun-style cooking method in which seasoned foods are cooked over high heat in a super-heated heavy skillet until charred on the outside.

Blanch
To boil briefly to loosen the skin of a fruit or a vegetable. After 30 seconds in boiling water, the fruit or vegetable should be plunged into ice water to stop the cooking action and then the skin easily slices or peels off.

Soups and Salads

Recipe Name: _____

Oven Temp: _____ Cook Time: _____

Ingredient List:

_____   _____

_____   _____

_____   _____

_____   _____

_____   _____

_____   _____

_____   _____

_____   _____

_____   _____

_____   _____

_____   _____

Recipe Directions:

Recipe Name: _____

Oven Temp: _____ Cook Time: _____

Ingredient List:

_____   _____

_____   _____

_____   _____

_____   _____

_____   _____

_____   _____

_____   _____

_____   _____

_____   _____

_____   _____

_____   _____

Recipe Directions:

Recipe Name: _____

Oven Temp: _____ Cook Time: _____

Ingredient List:

_____   _____

_____   _____

_____   _____

_____   _____

_____   _____

_____   _____

_____   _____

_____   _____

_____   _____

_____   _____

Recipe Directions:

Recipe Name: _____

Oven Temp: _____ Cook Time: _____

Ingredient List:

_____   _____

_____   _____

_____   _____

_____   _____

_____   _____

_____   _____

_____   _____

_____   _____

_____   _____

_____   _____

_____   _____

Recipe Directions:

Recipe Name: _____

Oven Temp: _____ Cook Time: _____

Ingredient List:

_____   _____

_____   _____

_____   _____

_____   _____

_____   _____

_____   _____

_____   _____

_____   _____

_____   _____

_____   _____

Recipe Directions:

Recipe Name: _____

Oven Temp: _____ Cook Time: _____

Ingredient List:

_____   _____

_____   _____

_____   _____

_____   _____

_____   _____

_____   _____

_____   _____

_____   _____

_____   _____

_____   _____

Recipe Directions:

Recipe Name: _____

Oven Temp: _____ Cook Time: _____

Ingredient List:

_____   _____

_____   _____

_____   _____

_____   _____

_____   _____

_____   _____

_____   _____

_____   _____

_____   _____

_____   _____

_____   _____

Recipe Directions:

Recipe Name: _____

Oven Temp: _____ Cook Time: _____

Ingredient List:

_____   _____

_____   _____

_____   _____

_____   _____

_____   _____

_____   _____

_____   _____

_____   _____

_____   _____

_____   _____

Recipe Directions:

Cooking Terms

Blend
To mix or fold two or more ingredients together, to obtain equal distribution throughout the mixture.

Boil
To cook food in heated water or other liquid that is bubbling vigorously.

Braise
A cooking technique that requires browning meat in oil or other fat and then cooking slowly in liquid. The effect of braising is to tenderize the meat.

Broil
To cook food directly under the heat source.

Broth or Stock
A flavorful liquid made by gently cooking meat, seafood or vegetables often with herbs, in liquid (usually water).

Brown
A quick saute, pan or oven broiling, or grilling method, done either at the beginning or end of meal preparation, often to enhance flavor, texture and or eye appeal.

Brush
Using a pastry brush to coat a food such as meat or bread with melted butter, glaze or other liquid.

Bundt Pan
The generic name for any tube baking pan having fluted sides.

Casseroles

Recipe Name: _____

Oven Temp: _____ Cook Time: _____

Ingredient List:

_____   _____

_____   _____

_____   _____

_____   _____

_____   _____

_____   _____

_____   _____

_____   _____

_____   _____

_____   _____

Recipe Directions:

Recipe Name: _____

Oven Temp: _____ Cook Time: _____

Ingredient List:

_____   _____

_____   _____

_____   _____

_____   _____

_____   _____

_____   _____

_____   _____

_____   _____

_____   _____

_____   _____

Recipe Directions:

Recipe Name: _____

Oven Temp: _____ Cook Time: _____

Ingredient List:

_____   _____

_____   _____

_____   _____

_____   _____

_____   _____

_____   _____

_____   _____

_____   _____

_____   _____

_____   _____

Recipe Directions:

Recipe Name: _____

Oven Temp: _____ Cook Time: _____

Ingredient List:

_____   _____

_____   _____

_____   _____

_____   _____

_____   _____

_____   _____

_____   _____

_____   _____

_____   _____

_____   _____

Recipe Directions:

Recipe Name: _____

Oven Temp: _____ Cook Time: _____

Ingredient List:

_____   _____

_____   _____

_____   _____

_____   _____

_____   _____

_____   _____

_____   _____

_____   _____

_____   _____

_____   _____

_____   _____

Recipe Directions:

Recipe Name: _____

Oven Temp: _____ Cook Time: _____

Ingredient List:

_____   _____

_____   _____

_____   _____

_____   _____

_____   _____

_____   _____

_____   _____

_____   _____

_____   _____

_____   _____

Recipe Directions:

Recipe Name: _____

Oven Temp: _____ Cook Time: _____

Ingredient List:

_____   _____

_____   _____

_____   _____

_____   _____

_____   _____

_____   _____

_____   _____

_____   _____

_____   _____

_____   _____

_____   _____

Recipe Directions:

Recipe Name: _____

Oven Temp: _____ Cook Time: _____

Ingredient List:

_____   _____

_____   _____

_____   _____

_____   _____

_____   _____

_____   _____

_____   _____

_____   _____

_____   _____

_____   _____

Recipe Directions:

Cooking Terms

Butterfly
To cut open a food such as pork chops down the center without cutting all the way through and then spread apart.

Caramelize
Browning sugar over a flame with or without the addition of some water to aid the process. The temperature range in which sugar caramelizes, approximately 320° to 360°.

Chiffon
Pie filling made light and fluffy with stabilized gelatin and beaten egg whites.

Chop
To cut into irregular pieces.

Coat
To evenly cover food with flour, crumbs or a batter.

Combine
To blend two or more ingredients into a single mixture.

Core
To remove the non edible centers of fruits such as pineapples.

Cream
To beat vegetable shortening, butter or margarine, with or without sugar, until light and fluffy. This process traps in air bubbles, later used to create height in cakes and cakes.

Crimp
To create a decorative edge on a piecrust. On a double pie crust, this will also seal both crust edges together.

Meat and Poultry

Recipe Name: _____

Oven Temp: _____ Cook Time: _____

Ingredient List:

_____   _____

_____   _____

_____   _____

_____   _____

_____   _____

_____   _____

_____   _____

_____   _____

_____   _____

_____   _____

Recipe Directions:

Recipe Name: _____

Oven Temp: _____ Cook Time: _____

Ingredient List:

_____	_____
_____	_____
_____	_____
_____	_____
_____	_____
_____	_____
_____	_____
_____	_____
_____	_____
_____	_____
_____	_____

Recipe Directions:

Recipe Name: _____

Oven Temp: _____ Cook Time: _____

Ingredient List:

_____   _____

_____   _____

_____   _____

_____   _____

_____   _____

_____   _____

_____   _____

_____   _____

_____   _____

_____   _____

Recipe Directions:

Recipe Name: _____

Oven Temp: _____ Cook Time: _____

Ingredient List:

_____   _____

_____   _____

_____   _____

_____   _____

_____   _____

_____   _____

_____   _____

_____   _____

_____   _____

_____   _____

_____   _____

Recipe Directions:

Recipe Name: _____

Oven Temp: _____ Cook Time: _____

Ingredient List:

_____   _____

_____   _____

_____   _____

_____   _____

_____   _____

_____   _____

_____   _____

_____   _____

_____   _____

_____   _____

_____   _____

Recipe Directions:

Recipe Name: _____

Oven Temp: _____ Cook Time: _____

Ingredient List:

_____   _____

_____   _____

_____   _____

_____   _____

_____   _____

_____   _____

_____   _____

_____   _____

_____   _____

_____   _____

Recipe Directions:

Recipe Name: _____

Oven Temp: _____ Cook Time: _____

Ingredient List:

_____   _____

_____   _____

_____   _____

_____   _____

_____   _____

_____   _____

_____   _____

_____   _____

_____   _____

_____   _____

Recipe Directions:

Recipe Name: _____

Oven Temp: _____ Cook Time: _____

Ingredient List:

_____   _____

_____   _____

_____   _____

_____   _____

_____   _____

_____   _____

_____   _____

_____   _____

_____   _____

_____   _____

Recipe Directions:

Cooking Terms

Crisp
To restore the crunch to foods; vegetables such as celery and carrots can be crisped with an ice water bath and foods such as stale crackers can be heated in a medium oven.

Cure
To preserve or add flavor with a soaking ingredient, usually salt, spices and/or sugar are used.

Custard
A mixture of beaten egg, milk and possibly other ingredients such as sweet or savory flavorings, which is cooked with gentle heat, often in a water bath or double boiler. As pie filling, custard is frequently cooked and chilled before being layered into a pre baked crust.

Dash
A measure approximately equal to 1/16 teaspoon.

Deep-fry
To completely submerge the food in hot oil.

Deglaze
To add liquid to a pan in which foods have been fried or roasted, in order to dissolve the caramelized juices stuck to the bottom of the pan.

Dice
To cut into cubes.

Pasta Dishes

Recipe Name: _____

Oven Temp: _____ Cook Time: _____

Ingredient List:

_____   _____

_____   _____

_____   _____

_____   _____

_____   _____

_____   _____

_____   _____

_____   _____

_____   _____

_____   _____

Recipe Directions:

Recipe Name: _____

Oven Temp: _____ Cook Time: _____

Ingredient List:

_____   _____

_____   _____

_____   _____

_____   _____

_____   _____

_____   _____

_____   _____

_____   _____

_____   _____

_____   _____

_____   _____

Recipe Directions:

Recipe Name: _____

Oven Temp: _____ Cook Time: _____

Ingredient List:

_____   _____

_____   _____

_____   _____

_____   _____

_____   _____

_____   _____

_____   _____

_____   _____

_____   _____

_____   _____

Recipe Directions:

Recipe Name: _____

Oven Temp: _____ Cook Time: _____

Ingredient List:

_____   _____

_____   _____

_____   _____

_____   _____

_____   _____

_____   _____

_____   _____

_____   _____

_____   _____

_____   _____

Recipe Directions:

Recipe Name: _____

Oven Temp: _____ Cook Time: _____

Ingredient List:

_____   _____

_____   _____

_____   _____

_____   _____

_____   _____

_____   _____

_____   _____

_____   _____

_____   _____

_____   _____

Recipe Directions:

Recipe Name: _____

Oven Temp: _____ Cook Time: _____

Ingredient List:

_____   _____

_____   _____

_____   _____

_____   _____

_____   _____

_____   _____

_____   _____

_____   _____

_____   _____

_____   _____

Recipe Directions:

Recipe Name: _____

Oven Temp: _____ Cook Time: _____

Ingredient List:

_____   _____

_____   _____

_____   _____

_____   _____

_____   _____

_____   _____

_____   _____

_____   _____

_____   _____

_____   _____

Recipe Directions:

Recipe Name: _____

Oven Temp: _____ Cook Time: _____

Ingredient List:

_____   _____

_____   _____

_____   _____

_____   _____

_____   _____

_____   _____

_____   _____

_____   _____

_____   _____

_____   _____

Recipe Directions:

Cooking Terms

Direct Heat
A cooking method that allows heat to meet food directly, such as grilling, broiling or toasting.

Dot
To sprinkle food with small bits of an ingredient such as butter to allow for even melting.

Dough
A combination of ingredients including flour, water or milk and sometimes, a leavening agent, producing a firm but workable mixture, mostly for making baked goods.

Dredge
To sprinkle lightly and evenly with sugar or flour. A dredger has holes pierced on the lid to sprinkle evenly.

Drizzle
To pour a liquid such as a sweet glaze or melted butter in a slow, light trickle over food.

Drippings
Used for gravies and sauces. Drippings are the liquids left in the bottom of a roasting or frying pan after meat is cooked.

Dust
To sprinkle food lightly with spices, sugar or flour. A light coating of food.

Entree
A French term that originally referred to the first course of a meal served after the soup and before the meat courses. In the United States it refers to the main dish of a meal.

Vegetables

Recipe Name: _____

Oven Temp: _____ Cook Time: _____

Ingredient List:

_____   _____

_____   _____

_____   _____

_____   _____

_____   _____

_____   _____

_____   _____

_____   _____

_____   _____

_____   _____

Recipe Directions:

Recipe Name: _____

Oven Temp: _____ Cook Time: _____

Ingredient List:

_____   _____

_____   _____

_____   _____

_____   _____

_____   _____

_____   _____

_____   _____

_____   _____

_____   _____

_____   _____

Recipe Directions:

Recipe Name: _____

Oven Temp: _____ Cook Time: _____

Ingredient List:

_____   _____

_____   _____

_____   _____

_____   _____

_____   _____

_____   _____

_____   _____

_____   _____

_____   _____

Recipe Directions:

Recipe Name: _____

Oven Temp: _____ Cook Time: _____

Ingredient List:

_____   _____

_____   _____

_____   _____

_____   _____

_____   _____

_____   _____

_____   _____

_____   _____

_____   _____

_____   _____

_____   _____

Recipe Directions:

Recipe Name: _____

Oven Temp: _____ Cook Time: _____

Ingredient List:

_____   _____

_____   _____

_____   _____

_____   _____

_____   _____

_____   _____

_____   _____

_____   _____

_____   _____

_____   _____

Recipe Directions:

Recipe Name: _____

Oven Temp: _____ Cook Time: _____

Ingredient List:

_____   _____

_____   _____

_____   _____

_____   _____

_____   _____

_____   _____

_____   _____

_____   _____

_____   _____

_____   _____

_____   _____

Recipe Directions:

Recipe Name: _____

Oven Temp: _____ Cook Time: _____

Ingredient List:

_____   _____

_____   _____

_____   _____

_____   _____

_____   _____

_____   _____

_____   _____

_____   _____

_____   _____

_____   _____

_____   _____

Recipe Directions:

Recipe Name: _____

Oven Temp: _____ Cook Time: _____

Ingredient List:

_____   _____

_____   _____

_____   _____

_____   _____

_____   _____

_____   _____

_____   _____

_____   _____

_____   _____

_____   _____

Recipe Directions:

Cooking Terms

Fillet
To remove the bones from meat or fish for cooking.

Firm-ball stage
In candy making, the point where boiling syrup dropped in cold water forms a ball that is compact yet gives slightly to the touch.

Flan
An open pie filled with sweet or savory ingredients; also, a Spanish dessert of baked custard covered with caramel.

Fold
To cut and mix lightly with a spoon to keep as much air in the mixture as possible.

Fry
To cook food in hot cooking oil, usually until a crispy brown crust forms.

Garnish
A decorative piece of an edible ingredient such as parsley, lemon wedges, croutons or chocolate curls placed as a finishing touch to dishes or drinks.

Glaze
A liquid that gives an item a shiny surface. Examples are fruit jams that have been heated or chocolate thinned with melted vegetable shortening. Also to cover a food with a liquid.

Grate
To shred or cut down a food into fine pieces by rubbing it against a rough surface.

Desserts

Recipe Name: _____

Oven Temp: _____ Cook Time: _____

Ingredient List:

_____   _____

_____   _____

_____   _____

_____   _____

_____   _____

_____   _____

_____   _____

_____   _____

_____   _____

_____   _____

_____   _____

Recipe Directions:

Recipe Name: _____

Oven Temp: _____ Cook Time: _____

Ingredient List:

_____   _____

_____   _____

_____   _____

_____   _____

_____   _____

_____   _____

_____   _____

_____   _____

_____   _____

_____   _____

Recipe Directions:

Recipe Name: _____

Oven Temp: _____ Cook Time: _____

Ingredient List:

_____   _____

_____   _____

_____   _____

_____   _____

_____   _____

_____   _____

_____   _____

_____   _____

_____   _____

_____   _____

_____   _____

Recipe Directions:

Recipe Name: _____

Oven Temp: _____ Cook Time: _____

Ingredient List:

_____   _____

_____   _____

_____   _____

_____   _____

_____   _____

_____   _____

_____   _____

_____   _____

_____   _____

_____   _____

_____   _____

Recipe Directions:

Recipe Name: _____

Oven Temp: _____ Cook Time: _____

Ingredient List:

_____   _____

_____   _____

_____   _____

_____   _____

_____   _____

_____   _____

_____   _____

_____   _____

_____   _____

_____   _____

_____   _____

Recipe Directions:

Recipe Name: _____

Oven Temp: _____ Cook Time: _____

Ingredient List:

_____ _____

_____ _____

_____ _____

_____ _____

_____ _____

_____ _____

_____ _____

_____ _____

_____ _____

_____ _____

Recipe Directions:

Recipe Name: _____

Oven Temp: _____ Cook Time: _____

Ingredient List:

_____   _____

_____   _____

_____   _____

_____   _____

_____   _____

_____   _____

_____   _____

_____   _____

_____   _____

_____   _____

Recipe Directions:

Recipe Name: _____

Oven Temp: _____ Cook Time: _____

Ingredient List:

_____   _____

_____   _____

_____   _____

_____   _____

_____   _____

_____   _____

_____   _____

_____   _____

_____   _____

_____   _____

Recipe Directions:

Cooking Terms

Grease
To coat a pan or skillet with a thin layer of oil. Virgin olive oil is one of the best to use.

Grill
To cook over the heat source (traditionally over wood coals) in the open air.

Grind
To mechanically cut a food into small pieces.

Knead
To work dough with the heels of your hands in a pressing and folding motion until it becomes smooth and elastic.

Loin
A cut of meat that typically comes from the back of the animal.

Marinate
Coat or immerse foods in an acidic-based liquid or dry rub, to tenderize and add flavor before cooking and eating.

Mash
To beat or press a food to remove lumps and make a smooth mixture.

Meringue
Egg whites beaten until they are stiff, then sweetened. Can be used as the topping for pies or baked as cakes.

Mince
To chop food into tiny irregular pieces.

Breads, Pies
and Cakes

Recipe Name: _____

Oven Temp: _____ Cook Time: _____

Ingredient List:

_____	_____
_____	_____
_____	_____
_____	_____
_____	_____
_____	_____
_____	_____
_____	_____
_____	_____
_____	_____

Recipe Directions:

Recipe Name: _____

Oven Temp: _____ Cook Time: _____

Ingredient List:

_____   _____

_____   _____

_____   _____

_____   _____

_____   _____

_____   _____

_____   _____

_____   _____

_____   _____

_____   _____

Recipe Directions:

Recipe Name: _____

Oven Temp: _____ Cook Time: _____

Ingredient List:

_____   _____

_____   _____

_____   _____

_____   _____

_____   _____

_____   _____

_____   _____

_____   _____

_____   _____

_____   _____

Recipe Directions:

Recipe Name: _____

Oven Temp: _____ Cook Time: _____

Ingredient List:

_____   _____

_____   _____

_____   _____

_____   _____

_____   _____

_____   _____

_____   _____

_____   _____

_____   _____

_____   _____

Recipe Directions:

Recipe Name: _____

Oven Temp: _____ Cook Time: _____

Ingredient List:

_____   _____

_____   _____

_____   _____

_____   _____

_____   _____

_____   _____

_____   _____

_____   _____

_____   _____

_____   _____

_____   _____

Recipe Directions:

Recipe Name: _____

Oven Temp: _____ Cook Time: _____

Ingredient List:

_____   _____

_____   _____

_____   _____

_____   _____

_____   _____

_____   _____

_____   _____

_____   _____

_____   _____

_____   _____

Recipe Directions:

Recipe Name: _____

Oven Temp: _____ Cook Time: _____

Ingredient List:

_____   _____

_____   _____

_____   _____

_____   _____

_____   _____

_____   _____

_____   _____

_____   _____

_____   _____

_____   _____

_____   _____

Recipe Directions:

Recipe Name: _____

Oven Temp: _____ Cook Time: _____

Ingredient List:

_____   _____

_____   _____

_____   _____

_____   _____

_____   _____

_____   _____

_____   _____

_____   _____

_____   _____

_____   _____

Recipe Directions:

Cooking Terms

Mix
To beat or stir two or more foods together until they are thoroughly combined.

Moisten
Adding enough liquid to dry ingredients to dampen but not soak them.

Pan Fry
To cook in a hot pan with small amount of hot oil, butter or other fat, turning the food over once or twice.

Parchment
A heavy heat-resistant paper used in cooking.

Poach
To simmer in liquid.

Pressure Cooking
A cooking method that uses steam trapped under a locked lid to produce high temperatures and achieve fast cooking time.

Puree
To mash or sieve food into a thick liquid.

Reduce
To cook liquids down so that some of the water evaporates.

Roast
To cook uncovered in the oven.

Saute
To cook food quickly in a small amount of oil in a skillet or frying pan over direct heat.

Miscellaneous Dishes

Recipe Name: _____

Oven Temp: _____ Cook Time: _____

Ingredient List:

_____   _____

_____   _____

_____   _____

_____   _____

_____   _____

_____   _____

_____   _____

_____   _____

_____   _____

_____   _____

_____   _____

Recipe Directions:

Recipe Name: _____

Oven Temp: _____ Cook Time: _____

Ingredient List:

_____   _____

_____   _____

_____   _____

_____   _____

_____   _____

_____   _____

_____   _____

_____   _____

_____   _____

_____   _____

Recipe Directions:

Recipe Name: _____

Oven Temp: _____ Cook Time: _____

Ingredient List:

_____   _____

_____   _____

_____   _____

_____   _____

_____   _____

_____   _____

_____   _____

_____   _____

_____   _____

_____   _____

Recipe Directions:

Recipe Name: _____

Oven Temp: _____ Cook Time: _____

Ingredient List:

_____   _____

_____   _____

_____   _____

_____   _____

_____   _____

_____   _____

_____   _____

_____   _____

_____   _____

_____   _____

Recipe Directions:

Recipe Name: _____

Oven Temp: _____ Cook Time: _____

Ingredient List:

_____   _____

_____   _____

_____   _____

_____   _____

_____   _____

_____   _____

_____   _____

_____   _____

_____   _____

_____   _____

Recipe Directions:

Recipe Name: _____

Oven Temp: _____ Cook Time: _____

Ingredient List:

_____   _____

_____   _____

_____   _____

_____   _____

_____   _____

_____   _____

_____   _____

_____   _____

_____   _____

_____   _____

Recipe Directions:

Cooking Terms

Scald
Cooking a liquid such as milk to just below the point of boiling.

Score
To tenderize meat by making a number of shallow (often diagonal) cuts across its surface.

Sear
Sealing in a meat's juices by cooking it quickly under very high heat.

Set
Let food become solid.

Shred
To cut or tear into long narrow strips, either by hand or by using a grater or food processor.

Sift
To remove large lumps from a dry ingredient such as flour or confectioners' sugar by passing them through a fine mesh.

Simmer
Cooking food in a liquid at a low enough temperature so that small bubbles begin to break the surface. A very low boil.

Skim
To remove the top fat layer from stocks, soups, sauces or other liquids such as cream from milk.

Cooking Terms

Steam
To cook over boiling water in a covered pan, this method keeps foods' shape, texture and nutritional value intact better than methods such as boiling.

Stewing
Browning small pieces of meat, poultry or fish, then simmering them with vegetables or other ingredients in enough liquid to cover them, usually in a closed pot on the stove, in the oven or with a slow cooker.

Stir-Fry
The fast frying of small pieces of meat and vegetables over very high heat with continual and rapid stirring.

Toss
To thoroughly combine several ingredients by mixing lightly.

Whip
To incorporate air into ingredients such as cream or egg whites by beating them until light and fluffy; also refers to the utensil used for this action.

Whisk
To mix or fluff by beating; also refers to the utensil used for this action.

Zest
The thin brightly colored outer part of the rind of citrus fruits. They contain volatile oils used as a flavoring.

Measuring

Measuring Guide
This equivalency chart will help you with any measuring you
do in the kitchen.

3 teaspoons = 1 tablespoon
4 tablespoons = 1/4 cup
5 tablespoons + 1 teaspoon = 1/3 cup
8 tablespoons = 1/2 cup
1 cup = 1/2 pint
2 cups = 1 pint
4 cups (2 pints) = 1 quart
4 quarts = 1 gallon
16 ounces = 1 pound
Dash or pinch = less than 1/8 teaspoon

Common Abbreviations
Some recipes use abbreviations. Here are some common ones.

t = teaspoon
tsp = teaspoon
T = tablespoon
Tbsp = tablespoon
c = cup
oz = ounce
pt = pint
qt = quart
gal = gallon
lb = pound
# = pound

CPSIA information can be obtained
at www.ICGtesting.com
Printed in the USA
LVOW04s0247081116
512035LV00016BA/702/P